From My Italian Heart to Your *Table*

TINA KYCYNKA

Tampa, Florida
Jodi K Costa, LLC

Copyright © 2026 TINA KYCYNKA
All Rights Reserved. Printed in the U.S.A.

Publisher: Shine Press
4522 W. Village Dr. #1294
Tampa, Florida 34624
Shine-Press.com | Jodi@Shine-Press.com
Shine Press is an imprint of Jodi K Costa, LLC.

No part of this publication may be reproduced, distributed, or transmitted in any form or by any means, including photocopying, recording, or other electronic or mechanical methods, without the prior written permission of the publisher, except in the case of brief quotations embodied in critical reviews and certain other noncommercial uses permitted by copyright law.

For speaking engagements, event invitations, bulk orders, and other author requests, please contact the publisher: jodi@shine-press.com

Paperback ISBN: 979-8-9937924-3-9
Ebook is also available.

FIRST EDITION

Shine Press offers book publishing and marketing services, focusing on high quality at affordable prices with an excellent author experience.

Contact us for more information about our personalized Spark Books, publishing packages, book marketing, and Bestseller Campaign.

Praises For

FROM MY ITALIAN HEART TO YOUR TABLE

"The dinner table is one of the most sacred places for our family. It is where we come together and where multiple generations express their love with shared recipes, traditions, and love passed down over the years. My grandfather used to say, in Italian, "Quando si mangia, non si parla" which means when we eat, we do not speak, but it is always the complete opposite. We discuss our day, our joys, our problems, our humor, and our love and passion for food and family. Tina embraces and understands all of this with her heritage, her roots, her traditions, and her recipes".

Guido Maniscalco, Friend

"As a restaurant owner of FlameStone American Grill, I've seen firsthand how true passion for food can elevate every dish—and that same passion comes alive on every page of "From My Italian Heart To Your Table". Tina Kycynka has captured the heart of Italian cooking, blending tradition with a personal touch that makes her recipes both approachable and inspiring. This book isn't just about food—it's about love, heritage, and the joy of sharing a meal. Her recipes feel like an invitation to her table—authentic, heartfelt, and full of flavor. This book is a wonderful celebration of Italian cooking and the joy it brings and is a beautiful contribution to the world of Italian cuisine."

Nick Pappas, Meat Up Restaurant Group

Dedication

To My Parents:

Without them raising me in a loving and wonderful home, always allowing and supporting me in all my crazy ventures, I would not be who I am today.

To My Nana and Grandmothers:

Thank you for teaching me so much in the kitchen and about the Italian culture. You truly birthed my love for cooking.

This book was meant to be published sooner. Then my mom needed more of me, so I set it aside. Every day, I wanted to finish it so she could read it. I think she was even more excited than I was. But life had different plans. At the age of 90, my mom, Micky Ruggiero, passed away. My truly amazing, beautiful mother... as you can imagine, my heart was shattered.

Then I remembered her excitement for the book. So, I pressed on. I hope she can see it from way up there in Heaven, and I hope she is proud and pleased with the end result.

Without my sweet mom teaching me, encouraging me, and giving me her passion for life and cooking, there would simply be no book.

♡ Thank you for everything, Mom. I love you so much.

Foreword

I was raised in France by grandmothers who cooked the way one breathes—instinctively, lovingly, and with profound respect for ingredients. Their kitchens were places of alchemy and storytelling, where wild mushrooms gathered in the forest met a jack rabbit from the garden, and a simple meal became a celebration of life itself.

Those memories never left me. They shaped my understanding that food, at its best, is not about recipes—it's about generosity, care, and the joy of sharing something honest.

As a chef, I've spent years chasing precision—refining flavors, mastering consistency, and teaching others to reproduce beauty on a plate day after day. But I've also learned that good food does not belong to chefs. It belongs to anyone with passion, curiosity, and the courage to cook from the heart. The only true difference between a professional and a home cook is repetition—the ability to recreate excellence every single day. The soul, however, is the same.

Tina Kycynka's cookbook overflows with that soul. Within these pages, you'll find the warmth of Italian kitchens and the music of laughter around the table. You'll see recipes that are deeply personal yet wonderfully accessible—dishes like baked olives, homemade gnocchi, lemon pound cake, and her family's treasured sauce. Each one carries the signature of a cook who loves not only flavor but the people she's cooking for. These are recipes

that smell like Sunday afternoons, that invite you to roll up your sleeves, to improvise, to gather loved ones, and to make a joyful mess in the kitchen. It's a book of real food for real life—vivid, heartfelt, and beautifully human.

I've actually had the pleasure of tasting Tina's food, "in real life" as we now say in this modern world. What I found was rustic elegance, taste, and a simplicity that is always complicated to achieve.

Cooking, after all, is not a performance. It's a conversation between generations. And books like this keep that conversation alive.

Chef Gui Alinat, CEC

Author of The Chef's Repertoire and Eat More Burn More

Acknowledgments

I would like to thank my dear friends Chris and Nikki. They truly encouraged me daily to write this book. They supported me above and beyond and prayed. If it were not for them, "The dream would still be a dream."

To my dear sweet friend Tina Hinton, thank you for opening your heart and home to me and supporting me, for helping me create the perfect book cover, and for using your beautiful home to truly capture my vision.

To Jeff Rosenfield, for your friendship and your gift of capturing my love for life and my Italian culture in your photography. You are one of a kind.

To my amazing friend, Paula Joy, to whom there would be no book. She believed in me one hundred percent, saw this book before I did, understood my vision, and has been there on the business side along with encouragement and prayer.

Without Shine Press my amazing publisher there would definitely be no book. God truly sent her into my life to teach me and help me create a beautiful book.

To my awesome children, Christina, Bradley, and Jordan, for always encouraging me to go for it. You always cheered me on in life and in everything I wanted. You believed in me, stood with me, and reminded me to do what makes me happy and to walk in the talents God gave me. I am truly blessed that you are my children.

To my husband, Drew, for being my guinea pig, eating Italian almost every day for twenty-seven years, and being a part of my big, fat, crazy Italian family.

To my family, who has always said, "reach for the stars." My sister, bless her heart, has put up with so much. From my "I'm going to do this or that", it never ended. What a trooper she is.

To my friends who saw in me what I could not, who prayed and spoke my dreams into existence, and who never missed loving and encouraging me. To all my girlfriends who always straightened my crown, as we like to say, and held me accountable in life and friendship. I thank you!

Contributors

Jeff Rosenfield

Debbie Belleau

Joan Kistner

The Dough Artisan

Lori Witkin

Marisa Santella

Rae Lesmeister

Chanel Christiana

Christina Schoenmetz

Tina Hinton

Veselina Lovanovici

Paula Joy

Italians don’t measure seasonings.

We sprinkle and shake until the spirits of our ancestors whisper,

“Enough, my child.”

Dear Reader, Kitchen Master, Tummy-Filler,

This book has been a long time coming. I have prayed over it, that my heart would be evident, that you will love the recipes, and that God's love would be found between the pages.

I am so excited for you to experience this book through great meals, a laugh, and hopefully, feel encouraged. Most importantly, my wish for you is to create wonderful memories around your table!

"To some, eating is eating." They cook to eat, just to nourish their bodies. I find cooking is my expression of love to others. I wrote this book merely to share my passion for cooking, but also to bring joy to others through a gift God gave me.

It is not just about cooking. I do hope this book helps you to create some great food, but even more, I hope it brings you a smile, fills your heart (not only your stomach), and reminds you to remember some beautiful memories with your family.

I pray it reminds you how special you are, and whatever your passion is, to embrace it!

Most of all, my hope is that this book tells you a story and that the love I have for life and my family is evident. You would feel a touch of God throughout the pages!

Much Love

Contents

How To Use

This book follows the tone of how family recipes have been handed down from generation to generation. You won't find calorie charts or nutrition facts here — just good food, happy memories, and dishes made with love.

These recipes come straight from my heart and my kitchen — meals that have filled our table with laughter, conversation, and togetherness. We Italians don't count calories; we just say, "Everything in moderation."

Before you start, take a peek at the Abbreviations & Terms and My Favorite Herbs sections. They'll help you pick the best herbs and make cooking much easier and more fun.

In the pages ahead, you'll find recipes for Tapas — little starters or sides to share — then entrees, and finally something sweet to finish your meal.

So, gather your ingredients, pour yourself a glass of wine or a cup of espresso, pick a story to read, and let's cook together.

I would love to see you making your first recipe. Tag me on social media (links at www.TinaKLife.com) with a photo or video using #tinaklife, or email me at TinaKLife@gmail.com

It warms my heart to know you are enjoying this book and bringing recipes from My Italian Heart to your table.

Helpful Information

ABBREVIATIONS

EVOO = Extra Virgin Olive Oil

APO = A Pinch Of (a little bit of), approximately ⅛ teaspoon

PKG = Package

MIN = Minute

Med = Medium

Dash = Same as "APO"

TERMS

Al Dente = Cooked to be firm when bitten

TAPAS = Little Dishes or Snacks

WEIGHTS & MEASUREMENTS

Cup Measures (US)

1/4 cup= 60 ml = 2 fl. oz. = 4 Table-spoon

1/2 cup= 120 ml = 4 fl. oz. = 1/4 pint

3/4 cup= 180 ml = 6 fl. oz. = 12 Tablespoon

1 cup= 240 ml = 8 fl. oz. = 1/2 pint

US CUSTOMARY / METRIC WEIGHTS

1/4 oz. ≈ 8 grams [g]

1/2 oz. ≈ 15 grams [g]

1 oz. ≈ 30 grams [g]

4 oz. ≈ 115 grams [g]

8 oz. ≈ 230 grams [g]

1 lb. ≈ 450 grams [g]

METRIC / US CUSTOMARY WEIGHTS

1 g ≈ 1/32 oz.

10 g ≈ 1/3 oz.

50 g ≈ 1-3/4 oz.

100 g ≈ 3-1/2 oz.

300 g ≈ 10-1/2 oz.

450 g ≈ 1 lb.

1 kg ≈ 2-1/4 lb.

LIQUID MEASURES

1 teaspoon (US) ≈ 5 ml (1/6 fl. oz.)

1 Tablespoon (US) ≈ 15 ml (1/2 fl. oz.)

100 ml ≈ 3-1/2 fl. oz.

250 ml ≈ 8-1/2 fl. oz.

500 ml ≈ 1 pint (US)

1 L ≈ 2 pints (US)

1 fl. oz. ≈ 30 ml

1 pint (US) ≈ 1/2 L

1 quart (US) ≈ 1 L

1 gallon (US) ≈ 3-3/4 L

TEMPERATURE CONVERSIONS (C > F)

300 C ≈ 570-575 F

290 C ≈ 550-555 F

280 C ≈ 535-540 F

270 C ≈ 515-520 F

260 C ≈ 500 F

250 C ≈ 480-485 F

240 C ≈ 460-465 F

230 C ≈ 445-450 F

220 C ≈ 425-430 F

210 C ≈ 410 F

200 C ≈ 390-395 F

190 C ≈ 370-375 F

180 C ≈ 355-360 F

170 C ≈ 335-340 F

160 C ≈ 320 F

150 C ≈ 300-305 F

140 C ≈ 280-285 F

130 C ≈ 265-270 F

120 C ≈ 245-250 F

110 C ≈ 230 F

100 C ≈ 210-215 F

90 C ≈ 190-195 F

RECOMMENDATIONS

Basil is best used in salads, sauces, and as a garnish.

Rosemary goes great with pasta, poultry, lamb, and even stir-fry. This versatile herb is also delicious in Christmas holiday cocktails and mocktails.

Thyme can be used fresh or dried in soups, vegetables, and to season meats.

Oregano is perfect for adding to olive oil dips and is also used in tomato sauces and on pizza.

Soppresata is a dry Italian thinly sliced salami. It is a dry-cured pork salami that comes from the region of Calabria, Italy. One of my favorite Italian bites.

When a recipe calls for salt, I prefer sea salt.

Cicchetti

[Small Plates]

Baked Olives

Serves 2 to 3

INGREDIENTS

½ jar Kalamata olives

½ jar large green Sicilian olives

½ jar black pitted olives

1 bulb fresh garlic, chopped finely

Italian seasoning, to taste

Olive oil, for drizzling

Crushed red pepper, a pinch

Sea salt, to taste

INSTRUCTIONS

1. In a small baking dish, combine the above ingredients, drizzle well with olive oil, and cover with foil.
2. Bake at 350° for 25 minutes.

Tina says...

If you love olives and salt, you will enjoy this simple Tapas. Oh, and have a big, fat baguette ready.

Goat Cheese Toasts

Serves 2 to 3

INGREDIENTS

Olive Oil (for drizzling)

Goat Cheese 1 small log

Fresh Basil (to taste)

Sundried Tomato 1-2 pieces per toast

Baguette 1 large

INSTRUCTIONS

1. Slice the baguette into thin slices, brush with olive oil (or butter), and toast under a broiler until golden.
2. Spread a thin layer of goat cheese on each toasted slice. To that, add small amounts of sundried tomato, drizzle with olive oil, and top with a beautiful, fresh, bright green basil leaf.

Tina says...

I love it when friends stop by just to say hello. These ingredients are usually in my kitchen, ready to assemble together over a glass of iced tea and some giggles.

Mini Italian Sandwiches

Serves 2 to 3

INGREDIENTS

½ lb. hot capicola (deli meat)

½ lb. soppressata (Italian thin dry salami)

¼ lb. Genoa salami

¼ lb. prosciutto

½ head of lettuce (to your liking)

2 large tomatoes

½ onion, sliced thin

Banana peppers (to your liking)

¼ lb. provolone cheese

Parmesan cheese, for sprinkling

1 large loaf Italian bread

Olive oil (enough to drizzle)

Red wine vinegar (drizzle to taste)

INSTRUCTIONS

1. On a cutting board, layer the ingredients. Coarsely chop the mixture as you would for a chopped salad. Drizzle with olive oil and red wine vinegar.
2. Slice the bread lengthwise and fill it with the chopped sandwich mixture. Sprinkle with grated Parmesan cheese and cut into finger-size sandwiches. Serve immediately.

Tina says...

If you are a sandwich person this is for you. Get that baguette ready.

Rice Balls

Serves 2 to 3

INGREDIENTS

2 eggs

¼ cup Parmesan cheese

1 tbsp fresh parsley

1 tbsp thyme

1 cup uncooked white rice

1 ½ cups breadcrumbs

2 cups olive oil

1 quart water

2 ½ tsp salt (split)

Ground pepper, to taste

INSTRUCTIONS

1. Mix Parmesan, parsley, eggs, thyme, half the salt, and pepper. Set aside.
2. Cook rice in water with remaining salt until mostly absorbed. Stir in egg mixture constantly. Cool for 1 hour or more.
3. Spread breadcrumbs on a sheet. Wet hands, roll rice into 1½-inch balls, then coat in breadcrumbs.
4. Heat olive oil to 350°F. Fry balls until golden, turning for even cooking. Drain and sprinkle with sea salt.

Tina says...

Traditionally known as arancini. Top with a dollop of basil pesto!

Bruschetta Figs-n-Blue Cheese

Serves 2 to 4

INGREDIENTS

Italian bread, 1 baguette

Fig spread, enough to cover the toasts

Fresh rosemary, to taste

Blue cheese, ¼ teaspoon (add more if you love it)

Olive oil, a drizzle

INSTRUCTIONS

1. Cut the bread into thin slices. Spread fig spread on each slice, then top with blue cheese and a few sprigs of rosemary. Drizzle with olive oil.
2. Bake at 350°F until the blue cheese melts slightly.

Tina says...

I love using fresh figs. Remove the tops and cut into cubes. Try it.

Antipasto

Serves 4

INGREDIENTS

Soppressata, ¼ lb., thinly sliced (important for flavor; applies to all meats)

Hot capicola, ½ lb.

Sweet capicola, ¼ lb.

Prosciutto, ½ lb.

Mortadella, ¼ lb.

Pecorino cheese, 1 wedge

Figs, 1 package

Roasted garlic

Grapes, 1 bunch

Anchovies, 1 tin

Sicilian green olives, ½ jar Stuffed blue cheese olives, ½ jar

INSTRUCTIONS

1. Keep in mind any potential food allergies among your guests. Confirm with your guest list so that you do not include anything that could trigger a reaction.
2. This is something I grew up eating a lot. The kids today call it "Char-Cu-Te-Rie."
3. Arrange your ingredients as you wish. The key is to make salty and sweet and all of your favorite things

Tina says...

Have fun with this one! The more colorful and varied, the better your spread will look and taste.

Stuffed Eggplant

Serves 2

INGREDIENTS

1 medium Italian eggplant

¼ cup Parmesan cheese

¼ cup breadcrumbs

SPICE BLEND

1 teaspoon oregano, finely chopped

1 teaspoon rosemary, finely chopped

Salt and pepper to taste

Drizzle of olive oil

INSTRUCTIONS

1. Wash the eggplant and cut it in half lengthwise. Scoop out the eggplant flesh, saving the shells for stuffing. Chop the scooped-out flesh into small pieces and mix with salt, pepper, oregano, and rosemary.
2. Fill the eggplant shells with the mixture. Top with extra salt and pepper, Parmesan cheese, and breadcrumbs. Drizzle with olive oil.
3. Bake at 400°F until the eggplant is tender and the cheese is golden, approximately 25 minutes.

Tina says...

A great side dish or in a light main. It should be no shock that I sprinkle a little fresh basil before serving.

Stuffed Zucchini

Serves 2 to 3

INGREDIENTS

1 large zucchini

½ lb ground Italian sausage

¼ cup Parmesan cheese

Spice Blend

1 teaspoon thyme, finely chopped

1 teaspoon parsley, finely chopped

1 teaspoon oregano, finely chopped

Salt and pepper, to taste

INSTRUCTIONS

1. Wash and dry the zucchini. Cut in half and scoop out the centers. Set aside.
2. Cook the sausage in a frying pan until just cooked, then drain any excess liquid. Mix the seasoning blend with the sausage and the scooped-out zucchini.
3. Spoon the mixture into the hollowed zucchini. Drizzle with olive oil and top with Parmesan cheese. Bake at 400°F until fork-tender, about 35 minutes.

Tina says...

What an impressive side for guests. Fresh herbs like basil or parsley add a burst of color and flavor.

Italian Skewers

Serves 2 to 3

INGREDIENTS

1 package (about 1 cup) cherry or grape tomatoes

1 package (8 oz) mozzarella pearls

⅓ lb prosciutto, sliced thin

¼ cup finely chopped basil

Sea salt, to taste

1 package short wooden skewers

INSTRUCTIONS

1. Alternate tomatoes and mozzarella balls on the skewers, then top with prosciutto scrunched into a star shape.
2. Lay the skewers in a shallow dish or bowl, drizzle with olive oil, add sea salt to taste, and sprinkle with chopped basil.

Tina says...

Italian skewers are meant to be customized! Try adding pitted olives, cucumbers, watermelon, Italian salami, or other cold cuts. Make it your own!

Sunday Dinners

Growing up, Sundays were always family dinner days. We ate together every night, but Sunday dinners were sacred. Home-cooked meals, never takeout—maybe an occasional pizza. Hours would pass while we talked, laughed, and ate. We might have heard the same stories a hundred times, but being together created a passion for cooking, eating, and sharing life with people.

Even as I got older and had my own kids, this tradition continued with Wednesday night dinners at my mom's house. Even now, if I'm alone, I light a candle, set out pretty dishes, pour a glass of wine, and make the experience special. Stop and savor the moment at your table—you won't regret it.

Roasted Veggies

Serves 3

INGREDIENTS

(Keep in mind these are just the vegetables that I love, but you can use whatever vegetables you like)

Small round potatoes

Fresh green beans

Small red and yellow sweet tomatoes (usually in a bag in produce) my favorite is actually the San Marzano at Trader Joe's, but any will do.

Two cloves of garlic, sliced into thin pieces

Sea salt and coarse, black pepper to taste

Sprinkle of crushed red pepper

Rosemary, Thyme, Olive Oil

Fresh grated Parmesan cheese

INSTRUCTIONS

1. Preheat the oven to 400°F.
2. Drizzle olive oil on a baking sheet. Arrange your potatoes and green beans on the sheet. Drizzle a little more olive oil over the vegetables and season with the spices. Add the sliced garlic throughout and sprinkle with fresh grated Parmesan.
3. Bake for approximately 10 to 12 minutes.
4. Remove from the oven and add tomatoes. Bake for another 5 to 8 minutes. I like my vegetables firm, but cook them to your liking. Serve alongside your favorite meal.

Tina says ...

Squeeze a fresh lemon over the veggies just before serving for an extra burst of flavor.

Insalata

[Salad]

Chick Pea Salad

Serves 3

INGREDIENTS

2 16-oz cans of chickpeas

1 small block of feta cheese

2 cucumbers

1 (12-oz) can sliced black olives

2 plum tomatoes chopped into small cubes

SPICE BLEND

1 teaspoon thyme, finely chopped

1 teaspoon oregano, finely chopped

Sea salt, crushed red pepper, and black pepper, to taste

Olive oil, for drizzling

INSTRUCTIONS

1. Rinse the chickpeas, cucumbers, and tomatoes well. Cube the tomatoes and cucumbers. Slice the olives if needed.
2. In a bowl, crumble the feta cheese and combine it with the cucumbers, tomatoes, and olives. Toss with olive oil, just enough to coat, and add the spice blend.

Tina says ...

I usually add a bit of balsamic vinegar as well. I love the sweetness it adds to this salty salad!

Tomato Mozzarella Stack

Serves 4

INGREDIENTS

3 large heirloom tomatoes (or your favorite)

2 small (8-oz) mozzarella balls

¼ lb prosciutto, thinly sliced

SPICE BLEND

Basil leaves for topping (approximately 10 leaves)

Rosemary, finely chopped (approximately 2 teaspoon)

Sea salt & pepper, to taste

Olive oil & balsamic vinegar, for drizzling (approximately ¼ cup)

INSTRUCTIONS

1. Slice the tomatoes and mozzarella into roughly ¼-inch slices
2. Layer tomatoes and mozzarella on a plate, creating at least two layers. Use prosciutto to complete the final layer and top with a basil leaf. Sprinkle with chopped rosemary and drizzle with olive oil and balsamic vinegar.

Tina says ...

This fresh, colorful salad is perfect as a starter or side. Serve immediately for the best flavor.

Tina's Tortellini Salad

Serves 4

INGREDIENTS

1 package cheese tortellini

1 medium jar Kalamata olives

1 large jar artichokes

1 (8-oz) dry salami, cubed

1 small can black pitted olives

1 small can Castelvetrano olives

1 package cubed cheddar

8 -oz mozzarella pearls

¼ lb thin strips of prosciutto

SPICE BLEND

1 teaspoon each: finely chopped garlic (2 cloves), crushed red pepper, parsley, thyme, rosemary, oregano

Olive oil, to drizzle and fresh basil leaves, to cover

INSTRUCTIONS

1. Cook the tortellini according to package directions. Rinse, drain, and set aside. Cube the cheddar.
2. Combine all ingredients in a bowl and toss with olive oil and the spice blend. Mix well, season with salt and pepper to taste, and top with fresh basil leaves.

Tina says ...

This salad is great to make ahead of time. Refrigerate to serve the next day.

Tomato Cucumber Fennel

Serves 4

INGREDIENTS

6 plum tomatoes or 3 heirloom tomatoes (about ½ cup when chopped)

2 cucumbers (about ½ cup when chopped)

1 fennel bulb (about ½ cup when chopped)

1 small white onion (about ½ cup when chopped)

Olive oil and white wine vinegar, to drizzle

Salt and pepper, to taste

INSTRUCTIONS

1. Chop the tomatoes, cucumber, fennel, and onion.
2. In a bowl, combine the chopped ingredients and toss with olive oil and white wine vinegar. Season with salt and pepper to taste.

Tina says ...

Makes a refreshing starter.

GENESIS 1:29

"And God said, 'Behold, I have given you every plant yielding seed... You shall have them for food.'"

Spinach Salad

Serves 2

INGREDIENTS

1 16-oz bag raw spinach

¼ cup walnuts

2 hard-boiled eggs

¼ cup fresh mushrooms

Olive oil and balsamic vinegar, to drizzle

Salt and pepper, to taste

INSTRUCTIONS

1. Rinse the mushrooms and spinach, and dry well. Slice the hard-boiled eggs.
2. In a bowl,. toss the spinach, mushrooms, and half of the sliced eggs with olive oil and balsamic vinegar. Top with the remaining eggs and season with sea salt and freshly ground black pepper.

Tina says ...

For extra crunch, lightly toast the walnuts before adding to the salad.

Wedge Salad

Serves 2

INGREDIENTS

½ head iceberg lettuce (divide into 2 wedges)

3 strips crisp-cooked bacon, crumbled (or more if you like)

5 cherry tomatoes

½ cup fresh blue cheese crumbles

¼ cup shaved Pecorino cheese

¼ cup chopped pecans

Salt and pepper, to taste

INSTRUCTIONS

1. Wash the lettuce, pat dry, and cut into wedges. Cook the bacon as desired, then set aside to cool.
2. Place a wedge of lettuce on a serving plate. Top with cherry tomatoes, blue cheese, Pecorino, crumbled bacon, and chopped pecans.

Tina says ...

This salad pairs perfectly with blue cheese dressing.

Italian Salad With Egg

Serves 4

INGREDIENTS

1 head romaine lettuce

1 bag arugula sprigs

1 bag spring mix lettuce blend

2 boiled eggs

¼ cup pine nuts

Olive oil and balsamic vinegar, to drizzle

Salt and pepper, to taste

1 large jar green Sicilian olives, pitted

1 small jar black olives, pitted

3 plum tomatoes

1 small jar artichokes

Pecorino cheese, for topping

INSTRUCTIONS

1. Wash the lettuces and pat dry. Hard boil the eggs. Drain olives and artichokes. Cube tomatoes and quarter artichokes. Shave about ½ cup of Pecorino cheese.
2. In a large bowl, combine all ingredients and toss with olive oil, balsamic vinegar, and salt and pepper to taste. Top with the shaved Pecorino cheese.

Tina says ...

This fresh, hearty salad is perfect as a main or side and can be customized with your favorite Italian ingredients.

Cherish Everything

The kitchen was always the heart of our home—pots clattering, sauce simmering, and love woven right into the air. Every weekend, and every Wednesday without fail, our family gathered around the table. While we chopped vegetables and shared stories from the day, recipes were passed down just as naturally as laughter.

The kids learned by watching and feeling, measuring not with cups but with intuition. We'd reminisce about old meals and the memories they carried, realizing it was never just dinner. It was connection, tradition, and the quiet magic of being together.

These are the days I wish I could bottle up and live again. Cherish your people—time moves faster than we think.

Un po' di questo e un po' quello

[This & That]

Gougada

Serves 4 people

INGREDIENTS

1 package fresh dough (available at most grocery stores)

1 small can San Marzano crushed tomatoes

¼ cup fresh basil

SPICE BLEND

Pinch of finely chopped rosemary, oregano, and thyme

Sea salt, black pepper, crushed red pepper, and garlic salt to taste

Olive oil, to drizzle

INSTRUCTIONS

1. Let the dough rise according to package directions. Finely chop the fresh herbs for the spice blend.
2. Lightly oil the bottom of an 8x11 glass baking dish. Place dough in the pan and spread it with your fingers, starting from the center and working out to the edges.
3. Drizzle with olive oil, spoon on the crushed tomatoes lightly, then add the spice blend. Top with fresh basil leaves.
4. Bake at 350 for 25 to 30 minutes, until the crust is golden.

Tina says ...

This was my grandmother's recipe. Serve warm as a snack or alongside your favorite Italian meal for an extra special touch.

JOHN 6:35

"Jesus said to them, 'I am the bread of life;
whoever comes to me shall not hunger.'"

Spinach, Potato & Eggs

Serves 2-3 people

INGREDIENTS

4 large eggs

1 medium potato, peeled and cut into small cubes

1 bag fresh spinach

¼ cup milk

½ stick butter

¼ cup grated Parmesan cheese

SPICE BLEND

½ teaspoon each, garlic salt, black pepper, thyme, parsley

INSTRUCTIONS

1. Rinse and dry the spinach and set aside. Boil the potatoes until soft and set aside. Mix the eggs, seasoning, milk, and Parmesan cheese until well combined.
2. Incorporate the cooked potatoes and spinach into the egg mixture. Pour into a hot, greased pan and cook as you would a traditional omelet.

Tina says...

Serve this Italian style omelet on crusty Italian bread for a hearty breakfast or brunch.

My Family Sauce

Serves 4

INGREDIENTS

1 16-oz can tomato puree

1 16-oz can crushed tomatoes (or 1 large can whole San Marzano tomatoes, cooked down)

SPICE BLEND

2 cloves fresh garlic, finely chopped

Pinch of finely chopped rosemary, oregano, parsley, and thyme

Sea salt, black pepper, crushed red pepper, garlic salt, to taste

¼ cup fresh basil

¼ cup shredded Pecorino cheese

Splash of red wine (about 2 light twists of the wrist)

Pinch of sugar

Olive oil, to drizzle (approximately ¼ cup)

INSTRUCTIONS

1. In a saucepot, sauté the fresh garlic in olive oil until lightly golden. Add the crushed tomatoes, tomato puree, and spice blend. Stir well, cover, and simmer for up to two hours or longer, stirring regularly to prevent sticking.

SUBSTITUTION NOTE

Use 2 lbs of fresh tomatoes instead of canned. If using whole tomatoes, crush them by hand first, then pulse in a food processor to your desired consistency.

Tina says...

I love to make this sauce with neck bones, riblets, meatballs, or pig's feet, which is a family tradition. First, brown the meat, then add it to the sauce and simmer. It turns out perfecto!

One of my favorite parts of this recipe is that it makes leftovers!

Jar Sauce People

Ohhhh, "Jar Sauce."

The first time I realized not everyone's family made homemade sauce, I was working at a place with a big kitchen. Sometimes, if time allowed, we'd take turns making a meal. One day, my friend asked if I was having lunch with them. I said sure. She said, "Okay, we're having spaghetti."

Ten minutes later, I came back from doing something and the "dinner" was already on the table. I asked, "Oh, you just made this?" She said, "No, it's Prego." I froze. Prego. In a jar.

I had never had jar sauce in my life, and I couldn't believe people actually ate this. I may have gasped a little. She asked me if I had ever had it. I said, "Never. Ever." We all laughed so hard. From that moment on, I became the one responsible for bringing homemade sauce to work.

And just so you know—I still haven't had Prego.

Dutch Oven Bread

Serves 4

INGREDIENTS

1 packet instant yeast

1 ½ cups warm water

3 ¼ cups all-purpose flour

½ tablespoon fine salt

INSTRUCTIONS

1. In a medium mixing bowl, add the warm water and whisk in the yeast and salt until mostly dissolved. Add the flour and mix until a sticky, wet dough forms. Cover the bowl with a towel and place it in a warm spot in the kitchen, or in an oven that is off.
2. Once the dough has doubled in size, turn it out onto a floured surface or parchment paper and shape it into a loaf. Score the top with a design, an X, or a few slits. Place the loaf (with parchment paper) in a Dutch oven.
3. Bake at 450°F for 30–35 minutes. Remove the lid and bake for another 5–8 minutes until the crust is golden brown. Cool on a wire rack before slicing.

Tina says...

Preheat your oven with the empty Dutch oven inside for best results.

NOTE:

If the dough is too dry, add about a tablespoon of water at a time. If it is too wet, add a tablespoon of flour until the dough reaches a sticky-wet texture.

MATTHEW 4:4

"Man shall not live by bread alone,
but by every word that comes from the mouth of God."

Frittata

Serves 4-5

INGREDIENTS

½ cup cherry tomatoes

½ cup artichoke hearts

1 small jar of artichokes

1 small green onion, chopped

6 slices of prosciutto torn into small pieces

1/3 cup Parmesan cheese

1 cup of shredded mozzarella

6 large eggs

1/3 cup milk

1 cup of arugula

SPICE BLEND

Chop together 1 teaspoon each: basil, oregano, garlic salt

INSTRUCTIONS

1. Preheat the oven to 425°F. Sauté tomatoes, artichokes, and green onions until the onions are soft. Pour mixture into a greased 9x12 baking dish.
2. In a separate bowl, whisk eggs, garlic, oregano, basil, prosciutto, mozzarella, and milk. Pour over vegetables. Top with Parmesan cheese.
3. Bake at 425°F for 20–25 minutes, until set and lightly golden.

Tina says ...

A super hearty breakfast or brunch for entertaining.

Turnips & Potatoes

Serves 4

INGREDIENTS

½ lb russet potatoes

1 large turnip

¼ cup milk

2 teaspoon butter (or to your liking)

Salt and pepper to taste

Pinch of garlic salt (optional, Tina style)

Fresh parsley for topping

INSTRUCTIONS

1. Peel, cube, and boil potatoes until tender. Drain and set aside.
2. Wash, peel, and cube the turnip like a potato. Boil until fork-tender (slightly longer than potatoes), then drain.
3. In a large pot, combine milk, butter, salt, pepper, and a pinch of garlic salt if desired. Add potatoes and turnips.
4. Mash everything together to your preferred consistency (Tina likes hers a little lumpy).
5. Top with chopped parsley and serve warm.

Tina Says...

I like to add a pinch of garlic salt for a subtle, savory kick.

Meatballs

Serves 4

INGREDIENTS

1 lb ground pork

1 lb ground beef

¼ cup milk

2 eggs

½ cup breadcrumbs*

½ cup grated parmesan cheese plus a little extra

2 cloves garlic, finely chopped

SPICE BLEND

1 ½ teaspoon salt

1 teaspoon black pepper

Pinch of fresh oregano, thyme, and rosemary

Olive oil for searing

INSTRUCTIONS

1. In a large bowl, combine all ingredients (*see alternate breadcrumb option below) and mix well. Form the mixture into balls and roll in extra parmesan cheese to coat.
2. Heat a little olive oil in a pan and pan fry the meatballs until crispy and browned on all sides.
3. If cooking in your sauce, add the browned meatballs to the sauce and let them simmer until fully cooked.
4. If not using a sauce, continue pan frying for 10 minutes or until cooked through, making sure the meatballs are evenly browned and fully cooked inside.

Tina Says...

For extra flavor, try this recipe with ½ lb. of veal.

Instead of breadcrumbs, break up a stale Italian baguette, soak it in milk for about 5 minutes, squeeze out the excess, and add it to your meat mixture.

Eggplant Stack

Serves 4-6

INGREDIENTS

1 Italian eggplant

2–3 eggs

½ cup milk

½ cup grated Romano cheese

1 cup breadcrumbs (or enough to coat slices)

Salt, pepper, and Italian herbs to taste

Vegetable oil for frying

Marinara sauce (Tina's favorite recipe or any marinara of your choice)

Ricotta cheese for topping

Fresh basil leaves for garnish

INSTRUCTIONS

1. Whisk eggs, milk, Romano, salt, pepper, and herbs.
2. Slice eggplant thin, dip in egg mixture, then coat with breadcrumbs.
3. Heat oil over medium heat and fry slices until golden. Drain on paper towels.
4. Preheat oven to 400°F. Layer sauce, eggplant, and Romano in a baking dish, ending with cheese and a sprinkle of garlic salt, salt, and pepper.
5. Bake 20–25 minutes until golden; add more sauce if needed.
6. Cool briefly, stack 3 slices per serving, top with ricotta, drizzle with sauce, and garnish with basil.

Tina Says...

This one is truly a family favorite. Serve it with love, laughter, and maybe a glass of Chianti!

A Family Favorite

When I first made this eggplant stack, my kids stared at it like it had just landed from another planet. "What is this purple thing with cheese on it?" my youngest asked, nose wrinkled. I laughed and told them it was magic—you had to trust me.

By the time the first layer of fried eggplant, sauce, and cheese hit the table, forks were flying, and suddenly that "purple thing" was gone in minutes. Now, it's a loved tradition. Every time I make it, the kitchen fills with laughter, the smell of frying eggplant, and enough Parmesan to make any Italian proud. It's messy, a little crispy, a lot cheesy, and perfectly imperfect—just the way I like it.

This dish reminds me that food isn't just about feeding the stomach. It's about gathering people, sharing stories, and making memories that taste even better than they look.

Roasted Potatoes, Carrots & Beans

Serves 4

INGREDIENTS

½ bag carrot slices (1 cup)

2 large russet potatoes, washed, peeled, sliced thin

½ bag fresh green beans

SPICE BLEND

½ teaspoon garlic salt

Salt and pepper to taste

½ teaspoon rosemary

½ teaspoon oregano

½ cup grated Parmesan cheese

Olive oil to coat

INSTRUCTIONS

1. In a glass-baking dish, drizzle olive oil and toss the carrots, potatoes, and green beans to coat. Drizzle with a little more olive oil, sprinkle with SPICE BLEND, and toss again to coat. Top with the Parmesan cheese.
2. Bake at 400°F for 25-30 minutes, tossing the vegetables halfway through to cook evenly.

Tina Says...

Perfect for a big family dinner. Serve with a smile and a sprinkle of love.

The Great Kickout

I wasn't around for this one, but it's a classic family story. Apparently, my VERY Italian grandmother was doing her daily housework when my grandfather came home with a friend. Just seeing him on the stairs was enough to rile her up. Grandma ran out, told the friend he was not welcome, and insisted Grandpa go with him. Rumor has it the friend might have had a little Mafia connection, but Grandma wasn't having it. He never returned.

Easy Peasy Pizza

Serves 4

INGREDIENTS

1 16-oz package of fresh dough

½ cup shredded mozzarella

3 or 4 spoonfuls of ricotta

½ cup pesto sauce

6 slices of prosciutto torn into small pieces

1/3 cup Parmesan cheese

1 plum tomato

1 ½ teaspoons of pine nuts

1 cup of arugula

½ cup fresh basil leaves

INSTRUCTIONS

1. Remove the dough from the package and place it on a floured surface. Rub olive oil on top of the dough and cover; let rise until doubled in size, about 1 hour. Roll out to the size of your pizza pan.
2. Brush the pizza dough with a little olive oil, then spread the pesto sauce over the top. Add mozzarella, arugula, and dollops of ricotta. Smooth out the ricotta and top with prosciutto. Sprinkle with Parmesan and additional mozzarella if desired, then add fresh basil leaves.
3. Bake at 500° for 10 minutes, or until the crust is golden brown.

Tina says...

Premade fresh pizza dough from Publix or your local grocery store works perfectly for this recipe.

My pesto sauce recipe is in this book under "Sauces."

I prefer using a pizza stone and use my knuckles to gently knead and stretch the dough to fit.

1 CORINTHIANS 10:31

"So whether you eat or drink or whatever you do,
do it all for the glory of God."

Piatto Principali

[Main Dishes]

Pasta Puttanesca

Serves 4-6

INGREDIENTS

1 box linguini (or any pasta you like)

Garlic, sliced thin or finely chopped (I like a lot!)

1 cup black olives, large and pitted

½ cup small capers

4 anchovy fillets (optional, but go big if you love them!)

Black pepper, parsley, oregano, to taste

½ teaspoon crushed red pepper

¼ cup fresh basil leaves (I like a lot!)

1 large can whole peeled San Marzano tomatoes

Extra-virgin olive oil

Handful of pine nuts

Freshly grated Pecorino cheese, for topping

INSTRUCTIONS

1. In a medium-large sauté pan, heat olive oil (about ¼ cup or less) over medium heat. Add the garlic, then anchovies and crushed red pepper. Stir for about 3 minutes.
2. Add the olives, capers, oregano, and whole tomatoes, breaking up the tomatoes with a spoon. Bring to a simmer, then reduce heat to low, cover, and cook for 30–40 minutes. I like my sauce on the thicker side.
3. Meanwhile, cook the pasta just under the suggested cooking time on the box. Before draining, add a splash of pasta water to the sauce. Drain the pasta and toss it into the sauce.

4. Add fresh basil and Pecorino cheese, give it a good toss, and serve in a fabulous bowl with extra cheese on top.

Tina says ...

This is a dish to love , laugh over, and get creative with—add your favorite ingredients and make it your own!

Family, Food, Fun

This dish is a hit with my family! The olives in the recipe are a must for us. I get asked to make this one a lot because it's quick, easy, and full of flavor. Every time we eat it, it makes us laugh.

A LITTLE HISTORY

Puttanesca comes from the Italian word PUTTANA, meaning "prostitute." The sauce is said to have been devised by prostitutes as a meal that could be cooked quickly between clients' visits. In our family, it was also known as a "poor man's supper" because you could use almost anything you had on hand. Anchovies or tuna were common, but you can really let your imagination run wild with this one.

Meatloaf with Potatoes and Green Beans

Serves 2

INGREDIENTS

2 lbs ground beef and pork mixture

2 eggs

¾ cup breadcrumbs (homemade is best)

Handful of stale Italian bread, soak it in milk, then squeeze out the excess

1 teaspoon garlic salt

1 teaspoon basil

1 teaspoon oregano

1 teaspoon thyme

¼ teaspoon fresh chopped garlic (optional, I like a lot)

¼ cup fresh grated Parmesan cheese (or more, to taste)

Salt and pepper to taste

1 teaspoon fresh rosemary for topping

Optional: 5 slices of bacon to take it up a notch

¼ cup goat cheese for topping

INSTRUCTIONS

1. Mix the beef and pork with eggs, breadcrumbs, Parmesan cheese, garlic, salt, pepper, and herbs. Form into a loaf and place on a baking sheet. Spread goat cheese on top and sprinkle with rosemary. If using bacon, wrap the meatloaf and drizzle lightly with olive oil. Bake at 350° for 50–60 minutes, checking at the 50-minute mark.

2. For the vegetables, wash and trim a bag of green beans and peel and slice 3 russet potatoes. Toss with olive oil, garlic salt, salt, and pepper. Arrange on a baking sheet and bake with the meatloaf for the last 30 minutes. I like my vegetables firm.

Tina says...

- Homemade breadcrumbs make a huge difference. Don't be afraid to get a little creative with your spices.
- Goat cheese on top is my secret for extra flavor.
- Wrapping in bacon takes it to the next level!

Proverbs 15:17

"better is a dinner of herbs where Love is,

then a stalled ox and hatred there within."

Ricotta Gnocchi

Serves 4

INGREDIENTS

1 cup all-purpose flour, unbleached

Note: You may need more-about 1 cup + 2 ½ tablespoons

1 ¼ cups whole milk ricotta cheese

½ cup Reggiano cheese, grated

1 large egg, beaten

¼ teaspoon salt

Nutmeg, freshly grated, a pinch

All-purpose flour for dusting

INSTRUCTIONS

1. Drain ricotta in a cheesecloth-lined strainer, weighed down with a plate, until no longer watery.
2. DOUGH: In a bowl, mix drained ricotta, Reggiano, salt, pepper, egg, and nutmeg. Add about ⅔ of the flour and fold until stiff.
3. Lightly flour your workspace, turn out the dough, and knead into a slightly damp ball, adding flour as needed. Divide into 4–5 pieces, keeping extras covered. Roll each into ropes the width of a finger, cut into ¾-inch pieces, and dust with flour.
4. Use a gnocchi board or fork to make ridges, pressing and rolling gently. Transfer to a parchment-lined baking sheet.
5. Boil in salted water, 2–3 batches at a time. When they float, remove with a slotted spoon and toss with your favorite sauce.

Tina says...

- The nutmeg is optional. My grandmother used it and I loved it so much. Just the fragrance brings back fond memories.
- Don't rush it. Making gnocchi is as much about the laughter and memories as it is about the food.
- Work right on your butcher-block counter if you have one—it makes shaping the gnocchi easier.
- Don't skip the nutmeg—it adds a subtle warmth that makes these extra special.
- Pesto or a fresh tomato sauce is divine, but this gnocchi can go so many ways.

A Gnocchi Memory

When I was little, making gnocchi with my Nonna was always an event. The kitchen smelled like fresh ricotta, nutmeg, and a little flour dust in the air. I would stand on a stool, tiny fingers covered in flour, trying to roll the ropes just right. Nonna would laugh and shake her head, saying, "No, no, Tina! Not like a snake—like a pillow for the sauce!"

We'd cut the pieces, roll them on a fork to make the little ridges, and lay them out on a floured towel. I always tried to sneak one before it hit the boiling water, and Nonna would pretend to be stern while secretly letting me taste.

By the time the gnocchi floated to the top of the pot, the whole house smelled like Italy. We'd sit down at the table, sauce dripping from our spoons, and somehow, each bite tasted like love itself. That's the magic of gnocchi—it's not just food, it's a memory you can hold in your hands and share with everyone you love.

Italian Stew

Serves 4 to 6

INGREDIENTS

2-3 boneless chicken breasts

5-6 hot Italian sausages

1 package pork chops (4)

1 bag fresh green beans, cleaned and snipped

Fresh garlic

Fresh rosemary, oregano, thyme

Sea salt and pepper

Olive oil

Originally, this was done over white rice—my kids love it this way today!

INSTRUCTIONS

1. Trim and pat dry chicken. Pierce sausages with a fork. Keep utensils clean.
2. In a sauté pan, heat olive oil over low heat, add garlic, and cook until golden. Brown chicken 4 minutes per side with Italian seasoning; remove. Brown sausages and pork chops the same way; remove.
3. Add browned meats to your prepared sauce in a Dutch oven or crockpot. Simmer on low for several hours. Add green beans during the last hour.
4. Serve over pasta or white rice.

Tina says...

This is one of my original recipes. Let this stew simmer slowly—the longer it cooks, the more the flavors blend.

A Different Sunday Meal

This stew started because I didn't just want another "bit of Sunday sauce," and I happened to have a little extra meat on hand. I wanted something hearty, comforting, and a little different from our usual meals. I remember my kids crowding around the kitchen, watching the sausages sizzle and the chicken brown, asking if they could taste a little piece.

Now it's become a tradition. On Sunday afternoons, the smell of the stew filling the house signals that family time is about to begin. We serve it over white rice, just the way my kids like it, and it's always gone before the last bite. This is what comfort food is all about—love, laughter, and a big, warm bowl of something made from the heart.

Chicken Cutlets

Serves 2

INGREDIENTS

2 boneless chicken breasts, cleaned and butterflied

2 eggs

½ cup milk

Panko bread crumbs for breading

Parmesan cheese, grated

Salt

Olive oil

Salt and pepper to taste

INSTRUCTIONS

1. Whisk eggs, milk, and a sprinkle of Parmesan for the egg wash. Spread breadcrumbs on a baking sheet for easy cleanup.
2. Pound chicken breasts thin, being careful not to tear. Dip each cutlet in the egg wash, then coat with breadcrumbs.
3. Heat olive oil in a frying pan and shallow-fry cutlets about 4 minutes per side, until golden and crispy and the internal temperature reaches 165°F.

Tina says...

Don't rush the panko—make sure every bite is fully coated. The crunch is worth it! I like to serve these with garlic mashed potatoes and fresh green beans.

Spaghetti, Garlic, and Oil

Serves 2-4

INGREDIENTS

1 lb. thin spaghetti

Three cloves garlic, thinly sliced

Crushed black pepper, coarse

Crushed red pepper

Olive oil

Romano cheese, shaved

Fresh basil leaves

A bit of fresh rosemary (optional)

Pecorino cheese for topping

INSTRUCTIONS

1. In a large sauté pan over low heat, coat the bottom with olive oil and add sliced garlic. Cook until lightly golden—do not brown.
2. Meanwhile, boil spaghetti until about 1 minute shy of done.
3. Using tongs, transfer pasta straight from the pot into the garlic oil. The pasta water will help create a silky sauce.
4. Turn heat to low, add basil, rosemary, salt, pepper, and a pinch of crushed red pepper. Toss gently.
5. Top with Pecorino and serve with crusty bread. Top with Pecorino cheese, grab a crusty loaf of bread!

Tina says...

The garlic makes this dish dance!

Fettuccine With Arrabbiata Sauce

Serves 4

INGREDIENTS

¾ cup chopped onion

1 teaspoon olive oil

Three cloves garlic, minced

¾ cup red wine (& some to sip)

2 cans peeled, diced tomatoes

2 tablespoons tomato paste

½ teaspoon Italian seasoning

1 tablespoon lemon juice

A pinch of white sugar

1 tablespoon fresh basil, chopped

1 teaspoon crushed red pepper flakes

1 ½ tablespoons chopped parsley

¼ teaspoon black pepper and a pinch of salt

1 lb. fettuccine

1 lb. cleaned and peeled, cooked shrimp

Parmesan cheese for topping

INSTRUCTIONS

1. In a large sauté pan over low heat, generously coat the bottom with olive oil and add sliced garlic. Cook until lightly golden—don't let it go too far or it will taste burnt!
2. Meanwhile, boil the spaghetti until about 1 minute shy of done.
3. Using tongs, transfer the pasta straight from the pot into the garlic oil. No strainer needed—Mom always said that little bit of pasta water makes the sauce silky.

4. Turn heat to low and add basil, rosemary, salt, pepper, and a pinch of red pepper flakes. Toss gently.
5. Shower with Pecorino and serve with a good crusty loaf. Heaven in a bowl!

Tina says...

The red pepper flake is the main character in this play.

Overboard

Arrabbiata means "angry," and yes, that's exactly how this sauce feels when it hits your tongue—bold, spicy, and unapologetically flavorful.

I discovered this sauce in Rome, and the locals laughed when I asked why it was called Arrabbiata. They said it was for the cooks who went a little overboard with garlic, chili flakes, and olive oil. For me, it became a signature in my kitchen, a sauce that wakes up your senses and makes any dinner feel like a celebration. I love serving it with shrimp—it's a little twist that makes everyone at the table smile, and yes, it's perfectly acceptable to sip a bit of red wine while cooking.

Sausage, Peppers, and Onions Hoagie

Serves 6

INGREDIENTS

Hoagie rolls

Package of hot Italian sausage (6)

Olive oil

1 large white onion

2 large yellow peppers

Garlic salt to taste

Parmesan cheese to top

Marinara sauce, optional

INSTRUCTIONS

1. Poke holes in the sausages and sprinkle with garlic salt. In a sauté pan with a drizzle of olive oil, cook them 6–8 minutes per side until nicely browned. Set aside.
2. Add peppers and onions to the same pan with a little more oil. Sauté until softened but still with a little bite. Return sausages to warm through—let everything get friendly in the pan.
3. Warm hoagie rolls at 300°F for about 4 minutes.
4. Assemble: sausage, peppers, onions, a generous shake of Parmesan, and marinara if you like.
5. Marinara recipe on page 46.

Tina says...

Heavy hand the Parmesan—every bite deserves it!

Lamb Chops

Serves 2

INGREDIENTS

4 lamb loin chops

One fresh garlic clove

Sea salt

Olive oil

Black pepper (coarse)

Fresh rosemary

3 tablespoons of butter

Salt and pepper

INSTRUCTIONS

1. Lightly coat lamb chops with olive oil, salt, and pepper.
2. Sear in a hot pan 2–3 minutes per side.
3. Reduce heat, add rosemary and butter, and cook 3–4 minutes more, or to desired doneness (145°F for medium-rare).
4. Serve with wilted spinach in olive oil and garlic.

Tina says...

A touch of butter and fresh rosemary takes these chops from everyday to extraordinary.

Italian Pie with Green Beans and Carrots

Serves 6

INGREDIENTS

1 box of Pillsbury dough pie crusts (2 sheets)

1 lb. of ground beef

Mashed potatoes (homemade, of course), approximately 2–3 cups

2 eggs

¼ cup milk (for egg wash)

¼ cup Parmesan cheese

Fresh rosemary

Oregano

Garlic (thin slices)

Sea salt, black pepper (coarse)

¼ cup goat cheese (crumbled)

Fresh string beans

Fresh whole carrots

Olive oil

Italian seasoning

INSTRUCTIONS

1. Prepare pie crusts as directed; grease a glass pie dish with butter.
2. In a frying pan, heat olive oil and cook garlic until lightly browned, about 4 minutes. Add meat and cook 7–10 minutes until browned; drain.
3. Combine meat with Parmesan, rosemary, oregano, salt, and pepper.

4. Line the dish with one crust, spread in the meat mixture, then layer mashed potatoes on top. Add crumbled goat cheese and black pepper.
5. Cover with the second crust, seal edges, and cut 4–5 slits on top. Brush with egg wash and sprinkle rosemary.
6. Bake at 350°F for 25 minutes or until golden brown.

Tina says...

This is comfort food at its finest. Pile the mashed potatoes high like a cushion for all the other tasty morsels to sit on.

Green Beans and Carrots

Serves 2-3

INGREDIENTS

½ lb. of fresh green beans, cleaned and snipped

½ lb. of carrots, washed

Olive oil

INSTRUCTIONS

1. Place them on a baking sheet and drizzle with olive oil, making sure to lightly coat.
2. Add garlic, salt, and pepper, and sprinkle with Parmesan cheese.
3. Bake at 425°F for 15–20 minutes. I like them firm.
4. Serve as a side for the Italian pie.

Tina says...

A simple side, but packed with flavor. Go heavy on the Parmesan!

Baked Ziti

Serves 4

INGREDIENTS

1 lb. of ziti

Optional: 1 lb. of ground Italian sausage

Fresh basil (save a few leaves for garnish)

1 8 oz container of whole ricotta cheese

1 10 oz package of shredded mozzarella cheese

Garlic salt to taste

INSTRUCTIONS

1. Sauté the sausage in a little olive oil with garlic salt for 10–12 minutes. Drain and set aside.
2. Cook pasta for 8 minutes, drain.
3. Layer sauce in a baking dish, then add pasta, ricotta, mozzarella, and sausage. Top with more sauce.
4. Add a little extra ricotta and basil on top.
5. Bake at 350°F for 30 minutes. Let rest before serving. Add extra sauce if needed, a pinch of crushed red pepper, and a little more basil—because why not?

Tina says...

Gooey, cheesy, and oh-so-satisfying! Invite some friends over and uncork some wine and great conversation.

Pasta with Peas

Serves 4

INGREDIENTS

1 lb. box of ditalini pasta

1 package of peas

¼ cup white onion, chopped fine

¼ lb. prosciutto, torn into small pieces

Salt and pepper

Chopped basil Parmesan cheese

Olive oil

INSTRUCTIONS

1. In a sauté pan, heat 3 TBL of olive oil and cook the onions over low heat for 3–4 minutes until softened.
2. Cook the pasta for half the time listed on the box. Drain and reserve 1–2 cups of pasta water—liquid gold!
3. Add peas to onions with ½ cup of reserved pasta water and simmer for 10 minutes.
4. Transfer the pasta to the pan and add another ¼ cup pasta water. Cook 5 more minutes, until al dente and happy.
5. Turn off the heat, add plenty of Parmesan and the prosciutto, toss well, garnish with basil, and finish with coarse black pepper.

Tina says...

Fresh green peas give this dish year-round appeal, making it just as delicious served cold in warm weather as it is enjoyed hot in the winter.

Rigatoni Sausage and Basil

Serves 4

INGREDIENTS

1 box of rigatoni

2 cloves of garlic

1 lb. hot Italian sausage

Spice blend

Tomato sauce of your choice

Olive oil

Salt and pepper to taste

Grated Parmesan cheese

Fresh basil

Ricotta cheese (optional)

INSTRUCTIONS

1. In a large pan, cook sausage over medium heat, pricking with a fork to release grease, until it reaches 160°F (15–20 minutes). Drain on paper towels.
2. Cook pasta per package directions, then toss with sauce and sliced sausage. Top with grated cheese, a dollop of ricotta, and a sprig of basil before serving.

Tina says...

A hearty, no-fuss dinner that never disappoints. Extra cheese and a little love mixed in are the ultimate key ingredients.

Sautéed Chicken + Tortellini

Serves 2

INGREDIENTS

3 boneless chicken breasts, skinless, cleaned, and butterflied

Salt

For the rub:

1 ½ teaspoons chili powder

1 ¼ teaspoons onion powder

1 ¼ teaspoons garlic powder

1 teaspoon smoked paprika (I love Trader Joe's)

½ teaspoon black pepper

Olive oil

2 tablespoons butter

For the tortellini:

1 package of store-bought fresh tortellini ½ cup butter

Garlic salt to taste

¼ cup fresh sage, chopped

Black pepper to taste

Grated cheese for topping

INSTRUCTIONS

CHICKEN:

1. Clean, butterfly, and pat dry chicken; season both sides with salt.
2. Mix paprika, chili powder, garlic and onion powder, black pepper, and basil. Rub chicken with olive oil, then coat in seasoning.

3. Heat olive oil in a skillet; cook chicken 5–6 minutes per side. Add 2 tbsp butter, spoon over chicken, and cook 5 more minutes until 165°F or no longer pink.

TORTELLINI:

4. Cook tortellini 2 minutes shy of package directions; drain.
5. In a pan, brown butter lightly, add garlic salt, sage, and black pepper. Toss in tortellini and cook 1–2 minutes.
6. Serve chicken with tortellini and top with grated cheese.

Tina says...

A simple but elegant dinner that looks fancy with minimal effort. Sage creates a homey warmth and unforgettable meal.

Eel For Dinner

I was a teenager when I discovered this "family tradition." I came home one day and went into the bathroom, and I heard my mom yelling. By the time I got there, I discovered some eel... in the tub! I shrieked, of course, and asked what was going on. My mom calmly said, "We're having eel for Sunday dinner." Apparently, that was their hangout space until the kitchen was ready. That's how I met my first eel.

Egg, Pasta, Artichokes, And Olives

Serves 4-5

INGREDIENTS

One bag of egg pasta

One small can of sliced black olives

One can of large artichokes, cut and quartered

Olive oil

Salt and pepper

INSTRUCTIONS

1. Cook the egg pasta according to the package instructions. Drain and place in a large bowl.
2. In a sauté pan, warm the artichokes and olives with a drizzle of olive oil for 2–3 minutes.
3. Remove from heat and drizzle generously with olive oil. Season with salt and pepper to taste.
4. Toss everything together gently and serve.

Tina says...

Sometimes the simplest meals are the most delicious. A little olive oil, fresh seasoning, and good company make this a favorite in no time!

Perfectly Imperfect Dinners

I grew up in a firefighter's family, which meant our dinners were anything but predictable. Holidays could be interrupted, regular meals pushed off, and schedules changed in an instant. But whenever we did make it to the table together, it felt magical. Every dinner was its own little event — different, unexpected, and somehow even more special because of it.

Not knowing when we'd get that holiday meal or that "normal" family dinner made the moments we did have feel treasured. And when Dad walked through the door and we were all finally together, everything felt exactly the way it was meant to be.

Salse

[Sauces]

Brown Butter Sauce with Sage

INGREDIENTS

6–8 sage leaves, torn apart (less for a less sage-y dish)

½ cup unsalted butter

½ teaspoon salt

Pinch of nutmeg

Fresh ground pepper, to taste

¼ cup grated Parmesan cheese

INSTRUCTIONS

1. Melt butter in a large sauté pan over medium-high heat for 3–4 minutes, until golden brown.
2. Add the sage leaves and cook for 2–2½ minutes until fragrant.
3. Stir in the nutmeg, salt, and fresh ground pepper (I like coarse).
4. Add the Parmesan cheese, stir to combine, and serve immediately.

Tina says...

This sauce is magic, simple, rich, and perfect with tortellini or gnocchi.
Why not drizzle it over grilled chicken and mashed potatoes.
Now, we're talkin'.

A la Vodka

INGREDIENTS

3 garlic cloves, minced

4 tablespoons extra-virgin olive oil

⅓ cup vodka

¼ teaspoon crushed red pepper flakes

1 28 oz can whole tomatoes

1½ tablespoons tomato paste

1 teaspoon kosher salt

⅓ cup fresh basil, chopped ¾ cup half-and-half

INSTRUCTIONS

1. Heat olive oil in a large pan over medium heat.
2. Sauté garlic until softened, then add red pepper flakes and cook 2 minutes.
3. Stir in tomatoes and vodka; cook 7–10 minutes until reduced. Add salt, pepper, and tomato paste; simmer 20 minutes.
4. Blend until smooth, return to pan, and stir in half-and-half. Cook 5 minutes, then add Parmesan and basil.
5. Toss with pasta, garnish with extra basil and cheese, and serve.

Tina says...

Have a heavy basil hand to use for garnish. It makes this creamy, dreamy sauce explode on your meal!

Lemon Butter Cream Sauce

INGREDIENTS

3 tablespoons butter

3 garlic cloves, minced

2 cups half-and-half

Zest of 1 lemon

2½ tablespoons fresh lemon juice

¼ cup grated Romano cheese

1½ tablespoons fresh parsley, chopped

Salt and pepper to taste

1½ tablespoons flour

INSTRUCTIONS

1. Melt butter over medium heat. Cook garlic 1 minute until fragrant.
2. Stir in flour 1 minute. Slowly add half-and-half, stirring, then season with salt and pepper; cook 2 minutes until thickened.
3. Whisk in lemon juice, then stir in parsley, Romano, and black pepper.
4. Serve over chicken or toss with pasta.

Tina says...

Make your meal sparkle with slices of lemon as a garnish.

Basil Pesto

INGREDIENTS

2½ cups fresh basil

⅓ cup pine nuts

½ cup Parmesan cheese

2 garlic cloves

½ cup olive oil

Pinch of salt and pepper

1 teaspoon lemon juice

INSTRUCTIONS

1. In a food processor, combine the pine nuts, garlic, salt, pepper, and lemon juice. Process until finely chopped.
2. Add the basil leaves and pulse until well incorporated.
3. While the processor is running, slowly stream in the olive oil.
4. Add the Parmesan cheese and give it a quick pulse to combine.
5. Serve over pasta, chicken, or as a dip for fresh bread.

Tina says...

Always taste and adjust the salt right before serving. You want that bright basil flavor to shine!

Mushroom Sauce

INGREDIENTS

2½ tablespoons butter

1 8-oz bag whole mushrooms (or more—can you ever have enough?)

½ tablespoon olive oil

2 garlic cloves, minced

½ cup dry white wine

Salt and pepper, to taste

½ cup vegetable broth

½ cup Parmesan cheese

1 cup heavy cream

2½ teaspoons fresh thyme

INSTRUCTIONS

1. Heat olive oil and butter in a pan over medium-high heat. Sauté garlic 2–3 minutes.
2. Add mushrooms; cook 5 minutes. Stir in white wine, scraping the pan 1 minute.
3. Add cream, broth, and Parmesan; simmer 3 minutes until thickened.
4. Stir in thyme, season with salt and pepper, and serve over ravioli, chicken, or your favorite dish.

Tina says...

Extra mushrooms mean extra magic!

Arrabbiata Sauce

INGREDIENTS

4 garlic cloves, thinly sliced or chopped

3½ tablespoons olive oil

1 small onion, chopped

2½ teaspoons crushed red pepper

1½ teaspoons oregano

2 large cans whole peeled tomatoes (I prefer San Marzano)

Fresh basil, to taste and for topping

Salt, to taste

INSTRUCTIONS

1. Warm olive oil over low heat. Sauté garlic 3 minutes, then add onion and red pepper; cook 2–3 minutes.
2. Add tomatoes, salt, and oregano; stir and add ¼ cup water if needed. Simmer 45 minutes, stirring occasionally.
3. Stir in basil and serve with pasta.

Tina says...

Turn up the heat. The spicier, the better!

1 TIMOTHY 4:4

"For everything God created is good, and nothing is to be rejected if it is received with thanksgiving."

Marinara Sauce

INGREDIENTS

3 cloves garlic, minced

2½ tablespoons extra-virgin olive oil

Sea salt, to taste

¼ teaspoon black pepper

Fresh parsley, chopped

Fresh basil, chopped

28-oz can crushed tomatoes

Oregano, to taste

INSTRUCTIONS

1. In a medium saucepot, heat olive oil over medium heat. Sauté garlic 2 minutes until golden and fragrant.
2. Add crushed tomatoes, salt, pepper, oregano, and parsley; stir to combine.
3. Bring to a gentle boil, then cover and simmer 30–45 minutes.
4. Top with fresh basil and your favorite cheese before serving.

Tina says...

A little patience brings out the best flavor—don't rush the simmer!
Oh, and Cento is my preferred crushed tomato brand.

Zuppa

[Soup]

Lentil Soup

Serves 4-6

INGREDIENTS

2 tablespoons olive oil

1 large yellow onion, diced

2–3 carrots, diced

2 ribs celery, diced

3 cups lentils (rinsed)

1 teaspoon ground cumin

2 bay leaves

6 cups chicken stock

2 cloves garlic, minced

Salt and pepper, to taste

½ lb. ground Italian sausage

2 teaspoons fresh rosemary, chopped

INSTRUCTIONS

1. Heat olive oil in a large pot over low heat. Cook onions 10 minutes until lightly browned.
2. Add garlic, celery, and carrots; cook 5 minutes. Stir in cumin, lentils, bay leaves, and stock.
3. Brown sausage in a pan, drain, and add to soup.
4. Cover and simmer 1 hour until lentils are tender. Remove bay leaves, stir in oregano, top with Parmesan, and serve.

Tina says...

This soup is even better the next day.

Chicken Pastina Soup

Serves 4-6

INGREDIENTS

2 ½ tablespoons olive oil

2 medium celery stalks, chopped

¾ cup onion, chopped

6 carrots, chopped into small pieces

6 cups chicken stock

Fresh Rosemary, chopped, to taste

1 cup pastina

½ chicken, shredded

Grated Parmesan cheese

INSTRUCTIONS

1. Heat olive oil in a Dutch oven over medium heat. Cook onions 3 minutes, then add carrots and celery; cook 4 more minutes.
2. Add stock, salt, pepper, and rosemary; bring to a boil, then simmer 30 minutes.
3. Stir in pastina; cook 6–7 minutes. Add shredded chicken, adjust seasoning, cover, and cook 15–20 minutes.
4. Serve with Parmesan and crusty bread.

Tina says...

This soup warms the soul and is perfect for dunking bread.

Kale Soup with Sausage

Serves 4-6

INGREDIENTS

One large bunch of kale, cleaned and chopped

½ lb. ground Italian sausage (hot, if you like)

3 large potatoes, washed, peeled, and cubed

2 tablespoons butter

3 cloves garlic, thinly sliced

6–7 cups chicken stock

1 small white onion, chopped

Olive oil

Salt and pepper

INSTRUCTIONS

1. In a large pot or Dutch oven, melt butter over medium heat. Cook onion until soft, then add garlic until golden. Season with salt and pepper and drizzle a bit of olive oil.
2. Add potatoes, chicken stock, and kale; simmer 25–30 minutes until tender.
3. In a separate pan, cook sausage 10–15 minutes until done. Stir into the soup and serve topped with Parmesan and cracked black pepper.

Tina says...

Adding greens to your diet adds years to your life.

Let's Bring Back Tradition

The table was scarred and uneven, its paint wearing thin, but it became a bridge — a bridge to happiness, love, growth, and the making of friendships and memories. In my childhood, meals around that table were constant. I can hardly remember a time when we weren't gathered there.

Today, it feels like no one has time for the table anymore. Everyone rushes in different directions, and watching that happen is hard, because the table is the heart of it all. It's where everything starts and ends.

Maybe, just maybe, one person believing in the power of a simple table is enough to bring people back together.

I sure hope so.

Dolci

[Sweet Things]

Lemon Pound Cake

INGREDIENTS

1 ½ cups all-purpose flour

½ teaspoon salt

1 cup unsalted butter, softened

1 ½ teaspoons baking powder

1 cup sugar

1 teaspoon lemon zest

3 large eggs

2 ½ tablespoons lemon juice (add more for extra lemon flavor)

1 teaspoon vanilla extract

Icing

2 tablespoons lemon juice

1 ½ tablespoons heavy cream

1 cup powdered sugar

INSTRUCTIONS

1. Preheat oven to 350°F and grease a 9x5-inch loaf pan. Whisk flour, salt, and baking powder; set aside.
2. Beat butter until smooth, add sugar, then eggs one at a time. Mix in lemon juice, zest, and vanilla.
3. Fold in dry ingredients; spread batter in pan and bake 50–60 minutes. Cool 45–50 minutes, then remove.
4. Icing
5. Whisk icing ingredients until smooth and pour over warm cake.

First Dinner

My Husband's First Family Dinner

We went to my parents' house for my husband's first official Italian meal. Let me tell you—my parents were definitely sizing him up. We all sat down, chatted, were having a great meal, and then... he got up. Yep. Thought it was a brilliant idea to move onto the couch mid-dinner.

Little did he know, in an Italian household, that just does not happen. My dad and mom both froze for a second, then directed him right back to the table. No excuses. Dinner was not over until they said it was over.

It's not just about eating—it's about the stories, the laughter, the back-and-forth in Italian, and making sure everyone knows that the table is sacred. Let's just say, he learned very quickly: in this house, you don't walk away from a meal until the table says it's done. And yes, the stories and laughter keep going long after the plates are cleared.

Fried Dough

Serves 4

INGREDIENTS

2 cups flour

2 teaspoons baking powder

1 tablespoon sugar

¾ teaspoon kosher salt

¾ cup warm milk

2 tablespoons unsalted butter, cold

Powdered sugar, for dusting

Vegetable oil, for frying

INSTRUCTIONS

1. Sift flour, sugar, baking powder, and salt in a bowl. Rub in cold butter. Stir in warm milk to form dough; cover and rest 15–20 minutes.
2. Heat 1 inch of oil to 350°F. Spray a spoon, scoop dough into small balls. Fry each ball about 1 minute per side until golden.
3. Drain on a rack or parchment and dust with powdered sugar.

Tina says...

You must try these with a shot of Sambuca. A grown-up treat!

Tiramisu

INGREDIENTS

1 8-oz tub of mascarpone

1 ½ cups whipping cream

⅓ cup regular sugar

1 teaspoon vanilla extract

1 ¾ cups espresso

4 tablespoons Frangelico (or chocolate/almond liqueur of your choice)

1 package of ladyfingers

Cocoa powder for dusting

INSTRUCTIONS

1. Whip heavy cream on medium speed, gradually adding sugar and vanilla until stiff peaks form. Fold in mascarpone until smooth; set aside.
2. Mix espresso and liqueur in a shallow bowl. Lightly dip ladyfingers or cake slices, then layer half in an 8x8-inch pan.
3. Spread half the mascarpone cream over them, add another layer of soaked ladyfingers, and top with remaining cream.
4. Dust generously with cocoa powder.

Tina says...

Put a paper doily on top of the dessert before dusting it. After dusting, carefully remove the paper to reveal the delicate design.

Honey Balls

Fills a dinner plate

INGREDIENTS

2 cups all-purpose flour

2 tablespoons unsalted butter

Zest of one lemon

Zest of one orange

3 tablespoons sugar

¼ teaspoon baking powder

½ teaspoon salt

1 teaspoon vanilla extract

3 eggs

Canola oil, for frying

Baking sprinkles

2 tablespoons orange juice

1 cup honey

INSTRUCTIONS

1. Cut butter into ½-inch pieces and set aside. Zest orange and lemon; measure 2 tbsp orange juice.
2. In a food processor, pulse flour, sugar, zest, juice, baking powder, and salt. Add butter; pulse until incorporated. Add eggs and vanilla; pulse until a dough ball forms. Form into a ball, wrap, and refrigerate 30–45 minutes.
3. Dust workspace with flour. Divide dough into 8–10 pieces. Roll each into a ½-inch-thick, 10-inch rope, cut into ½-inch pieces, and roll into balls on a parchment-lined baking sheet.
4. Heat 2 cups canola oil over medium heat. Fry dough balls until golden and puffy; drain on paper towels.

5. For the honey coating, heat honey and orange juice 1–2 minutes. Toss fried dough balls in syrup, then in sprinkles. Add extra honey if desired, cover, and leave at room temperature.

Tina says...

Our tradition was dunking the Struffoli (Italian title) in coffee, but honestly, they're perfect on their own. Remember, you can never have too much honey or sprinkles!

Christmas Honey Ball Tradition

Every Christmas, the kitchen smelled like a sweet, warm hug. The honey balls were the star of the table, and everyone helped arrange them. Tina's mom stacked the golden, puffy balls into a tall pyramid, each layer perfectly balanced.

Then came the fun part—decorating. Frosting was draped like garland, and sprinkles twinkled like tiny ornaments. The kids giggled as they added the finishing touches, sneaking a few bites when no one was looking.

By the time the pyramid was complete, it wasn't just a dessert—it was a sparkling centerpiece, a little edible Christmas tree that everyone admired before diving in. For me, this was the sweetest part of the holiday: laughter, sugar, and family all piled high.

Cannoli Dip

INGREDIENTS

1 16-oz container of ricotta cheese, drained

Optional: 6 oz mascarpone cheese

1 ½ teaspoons of vanilla

1 ½ cups powdered sugar

1 cup semi-sweet chocolate chips, small

Small waffle or cake cones, or broken cannoli shells for dipping

INSTRUCTIONS

1. In a bowl, combine ricotta and mascarpone (if using) and mix on medium speed until creamy.
2. Add the vanilla and powdered sugar, blending until smooth.
3. Fold in chocolate chips, reserving a few for topping.
4. Transfer to a serving bowl and top with the remaining chocolate chips.
5. Chill in the refrigerator for 15–30 minutes.
6. Serve with small waffle or cake cones, or broken cannoli shells.

Tina says...

Serve with dried or fresh fruit, either in individual bowls or on a plate with broken shell pieces.

We Italians Are Passionate

Growing up in an Italian-Irish family, I can tell you—we Italians live with a fire. It's impossible to ignore. A passion for life is woven into every gesture, every word, and, of course, every shared meal. We savor the world with all our senses. Life isn't something to rush through. We linger over it, celebrate it, even in the smallest moments. We live big, fiercely, and remind everyone around us that joy isn't a luxury—it's a choice.

Be filled with joy, my friends, and live life with passion.

Famiglia e Amici

[Family + Friends]

Italians don't measure seasonings.

We sprinkle and shake until the spirits of our ancestors whisper,

"Enough, my child."

My Mama's Kitchen

These next pages carry some of the most cherished people in my life. I'm honored to share the recipes they hold dear. My world would be far emptier without them. Thank you for filling my life and my table with joy, love, and laughter.

Italian Twist on Jewish Rugelach

By: Lori Witkin

DOUGH

1 cup butter – softened, room temperature

4-oz of cream cheese, room temperature

8 tablespoon Ricotta (not runny)

2 cups sifted Flour

FILLING

Any flavor of jam

1 cup sugar

1 teaspoon cinnamon

1 cup nuts (walnuts &/or almonds)

1 cup raisins (optional)

INSTRUCTIONS

1. Blend dough ingredients and slowly add flour. Use a potato masher to gather.
2. Knead about 10 times until a ball forms.
3. Divide dough into 4 parts, cover, refrigerate overnight.
4. Mix filling (sugar, cinnamon, nuts) and set aside.
5. Next day, let dough come to room temp.
6. Roll each part to ~9x9 inches, thin but not too thick.
7. Brush about 3 tbsp jam lightly over dough.
8. Sprinkle filling over dough (amount optional).

9. Gather dough at one end and roll into a log.
10. Brush top with milk/cream and sprinkle sugar.
11. Bake at 350°F for 35 minutes until top is browned.
12. Cool, then cut into 1-inch strips

Sicilian Caponata

By: Joan Kistner

INGREDIENTS

3 tablespoons avocado oil or any oil with a high smoking point (such as canola or vegetable)

1 medium-sized (skin-on or skin-off) eggplant cut into 1" pieces

3 tablespoons olive oil

1 peeled julienne white onion

2 thinly sliced ribs of celery

3 thinly sliced garlic cloves

1 cup Italian sliced green olives

1 cup Kalamata sliced olives (optional)

2 tablespoons capers

2/3 cup white wine vinegar

2 tablespoons sugar

1 cup crushed tomatoes

2 heaping tablespoons tomato paste

1 cup cherry or grape tomatoes, sliced in half

2 tablespoons chopped fresh basil

Sea salt & Pepper to taste

INSTRUCTIONS

1. Heat avocado oil in a large pan over high heat until smoking. Sauté eggplant 1–2 minutes until browned but firm; drain on paper towels.

2. Heat olive oil over medium heat, sauté onions and celery 8–10 minutes until lightly caramelized. Add garlic 30–45 seconds.
3. Stir in olives, capers, vinegar, and sugar; cook 3–4 minutes. Add crushed tomatoes and tomato paste; cook until thickened.
4. Add cherry tomatoes, eggplant, basil, salt, and pepper. Serve warm, room temperature, or cold. Optional: add pine nuts or anchovies.
5. Refrigerate until use; does not freeze well.
6. After my family visited Marsala, Sicily, I brought home the recipe for this Sicilian specialty. It can be served as a side to any dish, a sandwich topping, or as a snack on crostini.

Mediterranean Style Fish

By: Marisa Mauriello Santella

INGREDIENTS

Mild fish seasoned with salt and pepper - mahi, snapper, shrimp work great

Olive oil

Garlic, shallots, and alamata olives

Greens - arugula, spinach, kale (whatever I have in the garden)

Sauce Option 1: Toss tomatoes, basil, garlic, and shallots/onion with olive oil; roast until blistered. Puree for sauce.

Sauce Option 2: Sauté garlic and shallots in olive oil. Add canned tomatoes, basil or Italian seasoning, salt, pepper, and olives; simmer until soft. Use as-is or puree.

Sauté garlic and shallots with greens until wilted; remove. Cook seasoned fish in the same pan, adding oil if needed. Return greens, top with sauce, cover, and let rest off heat. Serve over rice or pasta.

Deb's Vietnamese Crescent Cookies

By: Debbie Belleau

INGREDIENTS

2½ lb butter

¼ cup granulated sugar

2 cups flour

1 teaspoon Vanilla

Confections sugar

INSTRUCTIONS

1. Preheat oven to 350. Room temperature butter. Add sugar, flour and vanilla and mix thoroughly.
2. Shape into delicate crescents about 2 inches long about 1/2 inch wide and thick.
3. Bake on ungreased cookie sheet for about 30 min, until lightly browned. Cool, and then roll in confection sugar (twice)
4. Makes about 35 cookies

Grape Leaves

By: Veselina Lovanovici

INGREDIENTS

2 Medium onions finely chopped

3 cloves of garlic minced

1/2 of cup rice

1 teaspoon salt 1-2 teaspoon ground black pepper

2 teaspoon finely chopped parsley

1 teaspoon finely chopped basil

1 teaspoon chopped mint

1 egg

2 teaspoon water

INSTRUCTIONS

Mix everything together in bowl. If using fresh grape or collard greens blanch them first and drain the excess water.

Start rolling (see like the picture) arrange the rolls in a pot.

Mix 1 teaspoon tomato paste with 2 cups water and salt to taste. Pour the liquid over the rolls just enough to cover it. Place a plate on top so the rolls don't float, cover with a lid and cook on low heat for about 2 hours.

The meat and the rice will absorb most of the liquid. Serve with sour cream and bread.

CHEF NOTE:

Best to use fresh tender leaves. If you use leaves from the jar, soak in water overnight. I used collard greens or cabbage. First, you will need 1 lb. of ground meat (beef, turkey, pork, and chicken are all good in various combinations. Or just one of the above. The beef should be 80 %, no leaner than that.

Cinnamon Applesauce from The Farm

By: Jamie Saffron (Old Glory Homestead)

INGREDIENTS

3 lbs organic gala apples

1teaspoon Saigon cinnamon

1½ tablespoons freshly squeezed lemon

INSTRUCTIONS

1. Peel and chop apples into small cubed pieces. Using a apple peeler will save time.
2. Add chopped apples into a Dutch oven, top with cinnamon and a fresh squeezed lemon juice.
3. Cook on medium heat covered for about 10 minutes until the apple mixture begins to bubble and simmer. Turn heat to lowest setting and simmer for 1-1 ½ hours stirring occasionally.
4. Once the apple mixture has decreased in size by 50%, add to a stand up mixer or use an immersion blender. Blend to your desired consistency. Double or triple recipe for canning.
5. Devour this warm, cold, or over pork chops.
6. It's the family fave here at our farm.

Olive Rosemary Bread

By: Istvan Molnar, The Dough Artesian

INGREDIENTS

28 -oz high gluten flour

8 -oz whole wheat flour

8 -oz starter

2 tablespoons salt

¾ cup green or black olives

1 tablespoon of fresh rosemary

3 ½ cups of water

INSTRUCTIONS

1. In a large bowl, dissolve 8 oz starter in 24 oz warm water (reserve remaining starter). Add 28 oz bread flour and 7 oz whole wheat flour; mix until no dry flour remains. Cover and rest 25–40 minutes.
2. Add salt, 1 oz warm water, olives, and rosemary; mix until incorporated. Cover and let rise 30 minutes in a warm spot (75–80°F). Perform folds every 30 minutes for 2½ hours (lift and fold each side), until dough is billowy and rises 20–30%.
3. Turn dough onto a floured surface, dust top with flour, divide in two, flip flour side down, fold onto itself, and rest 30 minutes.
4. Line two proofing baskets with floured towels. Lightly dust dough, flip flour side down, fold corners toward center, then flip seam side down and shape into tight balls. Place seam side up in baskets, cover, and let rise 3–4 hours.
5. 30 minutes before baking, heat Dutch oven to 500°F. Place one loaf seam side down, score top, cover, and bake 450°F 20 minutes. Remove lid; bake 20 more minutes until deep golden. Cool on wire rack at least 15 minutes.
6. Repeat with second loaf.

Deb's Lasagna

By: Debbie Belleau

INGREDIENTS

SAUCE

3 cans Tuttorosso tomato purée

1 can Tuttorosso tomato sauce

3 tubes Cento tomato paste

Salt & pepper to taste

Lawry's coarse ground garlic with parsley to taste

Parsley

1 lb hot Italian sausage

Pork riblets

MEATBALLS

⅔ lb ground beef (80% lean) + ⅓ lb ground pork

Locatelli Pecorino Romano (grated)

1 egg

Salt & pepper to taste

Lawry's coarse ground garlic with parsley to taste

Parsley

Italian bread (stale is best, small hoagie roll size)

LASAGNA

Ronzoni lasagna noodles

3 lbs ricotta (firm, not watery)

2 lbs mozzarella

Locatelli Pecorino Romano (grated)

INSTRUCTIONS

Sauce

1. In a large pot, cook hot Italian sausage. Season pork with salt, pepper, garlic, and parsley; cook in the same pot—don't drain drippings.
2. Add tomato purée, sauce, paste, ½ can water, plus more seasoning.
3. Simmer 3–5 hours, adding water if too thick; stir every 15 minutes.
4. Add meatballs for the last 2 hours of simmering.

Meatballs

5. Soak Italian bread in water, squeeze out excess.
6. Mix beef, pork, Romano, egg, seasoning, parsley, and bread.
7. Form small balls and fry until golden. Refrigerate until adding to sauce.

Lasagna

8. Cook noodles per package, drain, and air dry.
9. Spread sauce in baking pan. Layer noodles, half ricotta, meatballs, mozzarella, Romano, and parsley. Repeat layers.
10. Finish with noodles, sauce, mozzarella, Romano, and parsley.
11. Cover loosely with foil and bake at 350°F:
12. 1 hour if ingredients are warm
13. Up to 2 hours if cold
14. If refrigerated, bring to room temp 1–2 hours before baking
15. Let rest 30–60 minutes before serving.

I learned to cook from my great-grandmother, grandmother, and mom. I don't measure—everything is by texture, feel, and smell. Trust yourself with the salt, pepper, garlic, and parsley. And yes, I use a heavy hand with Locatelli Pecorino Romano... but it works!

Smoked Fish Cakes

By: Rae Lesmeister

INGREDIENTS

4 green onions, thinly sliced

1/4 cup finely chopped green sweet pepper

1/4 cup finely chopped sweet red pepper

1/4 cup mayonnaise

1/4 cup Creole mustard

1 clove garlic, minced

1 -2 tablespoons lemon juice

2 tablespoons capers, drained

1 teaspoon Old Bay® Seasoning

1/8 teaspoon cayenne pepper

1 lb. smoked trout, whitefish or salmon, flaked, with skin and bones removed (3-1/2 cups)

1 cup panko (Japanese-style bread crumbs) or soft French bread crumbs

2 tablespoons olive oil or vegetable oil

Lemon wedges (optional)

INSTRUCTIONS

1. In a large bowl combine the peppers, onions, mayo, mustard, garlic capers, lemon juice, when mixed add bread crumbs and fish. Mix it up well. Form into cakes.
2. Heat olive oil in a pan over medium. Cook cakes 5-6 min per side until golden brown.
3. Serve over a bed of arugula drizzle with dressing and top with a fresh lemon wedge.

4. The “Farm to Table” movement has great appeal because it’s good for both the environment and the palate. In my case, it’s more of a “Trout to Table” experience.
5. I love this recipe because it lets me share the bounty from a day of fishing on Lake Superior with my friends and family. Here’s how my husband and I turn a day on the water into a meal to share with loved ones. First, we clean the fish and brine it in brown sugar and salt. The next day, we cold smoke our trout (though you can easily buy smoked trout if you prefer).
6. After smoking, I make trout cakes and add a few special touches. I serve them over a bed of greens with a lemon vinaigrette and a dollop of sriracha mayonnaise on top, and always with love.

Chorizo Sausage

By: Chanel

INGREDIENTS:

½ bottle red wine

7 garlic cloves

2 tablespoons of cornstarch

Salt and pepper to taste

½ cup OVOO

For sides:

1 large potato

1 small broccoli, Rabe

Red Hot chili pepper to taste

Parsley

INSTRUCTIONS:

1. Braise chorizos in wine over medium heat along with the 6 garlic cloves. After about 35 to 40 minutes of braising, remove the chorizo and whisk in the cornstarch. Put chorizo's back in sauce.

POTATOES

2. Slice potatoes thin. Roast in olive oil until fork tender and golden brown salt and pepper to taste.

BROCCOLI RABE

3. Sauté broccoli, rabe in olive oil and garlic. Add sliced red hot chili peppers to taste. When done, plate and garnish everything with chop parsley.

The Circle of Traditions

Keeping my family traditions alive isn't just about repeating what my parents and grandparents did. It's about carrying their love and stories forward in the way we gather around the table, laugh a little too loud, share meals, and pass down recipes for future generations.

Every Sunday dinner, every holiday, every little ritual is a thread connecting me to those who came before and keeping their spirit alive. May the next generation feel the same sense of home, belonging, and love that shaped me.

From My Daughter

As a child, I have so many fond memories of cooking with my Mom and enjoying all of her favorites, made with so much love. My earliest memories of cooking with her started in my grandparents' log cabin during the holidays. I would put on my Nana's apron and help Grandpa with the mashed potatoes. That was one of his specialties. He would always make sure we added a turnip for good luck in health, and somehow, they were perfect every time. My uncle Rudy would even make mashed potato sandwiches for his long ride home.

I would then help Grandma with the sauce, although I was always in trouble for sneaking tastes. Later, I helped my Mom in every way I could, from learning the art of the perfect eggplant slice to making the table look just right. This was the standard "holiday chaos" in the kitchen that I loved, and now I hold it even closer to my heart as I get older.

As for my Mom cooking for me, those memories began in my childhood. It was simple things I may have taken for granted back then. She would make one of my favorites, Farina on the stove, with just the perfect amount of cinnamon and brown sugar. Still one of my favorites today. If you ask her, she will say my favorite was pancakes and bananas because that's what I loved as a toddler. I had to break that bad news recently that I actually disliked that as an adult, but she still insists it was my favorite.

Even now, as a 41-year-old married woman, my Mom still helps me cook. Usually through texts or panicked calls when I am at the store and can't remember exactly what I need for my Italian stew or Ropa Vieja. She always reassures me: I do know, just breathe, and always cook my meals with love - it's the most important ingredient. I have to confess that statement is true.

The love she puts into her culinary masterpieces is always felt. She has always been there to create something with love for me on my toughest days. Thank you, Mom, for all the wonderful memories of being in the kitchen, the most magical place on earth, with our family. I will truly cherish these forever. I love you.

Facts + Tips

Did you know?

- Chickpeas and almonds contain almost as much protein as steak. While 100g of steak has about 25g of protein, the same amount of chickpeas has 21g, and almonds pack a whopping 28g!
- Pistachios aren't technically nuts—they're a drupe, a fruit in the same family as cherries, peaches, and olives. They're rich in protein, fiber, vitamins, and minerals, improve digestion, and contain omega-3s that can help lower blood pressure.
- Caesar salad didn't originate in Italy—it was invented in Tijuana, Mexico, in 1927. Chef Caesar Cardini tossed together lettuce and a few ingredients he had on hand for dinner guests, and salad history was made. Source: eatfirst.com

Cheese, Please

Some of my favorite cheeses: Ricotta, Mascarpone, Pecorino Reggiano—and yes, a blue cheese is always welcome. Here's a quick guide on what I love and how I use them:

- **Ricotta:** Smooth and creamy, perfect for pastas, toppings, or fillings. Honestly, I could eat it straight off the spoon.
- **Pecorino Reggiano:** Similar to Parmesan, great in tomato sauces, on salads, or even pizza. There's a place for it everywhere.
- **Parmesan:** Hard, salty, and nutty—perfect for finishing pastas or sprinkling on veggies.
- **Asiago:** Hard and nutty with a slight sharpness; excellent on baked dishes.
- **Provolone:** Melts beautifully, great on hoagies or baked casseroles.
- **Mascarpone:** Creamy and rich, wonderful in desserts or creamy pasta dishes.
- **Gorgonzola:** A versatile blue cheese—sweet or spicy—used in salads, pasta, or pizza. I even add it to one of my meatloaf recipes.

- **Burrata:** My personal favorite, though honestly, every cheese is a favorite. Creamy, soft, slightly sweet, best at room temperature on toasted bread or pizza.

Don't be afraid to try new cheeses—you'll be pleasantly surprised.

The 20/20/20 Rule for Wine

- **Step 1:** Whites—take them out of the fridge 20 minutes before serving.
- **Step 2:** Reds—chill in the fridge for up to 20 minutes before serving.
- **Step 3:** After 20 minutes in the glass, your wine is perfectly aerated and ready to savor.

This trio of 20s will elevate your wine experience every time.

My Wine Favorites and Pairings

- Cabernet Sauvignon: Well-bodied and dry, pairs beautifully with steak and red meats. Also great in sauces.
- Pinot Noir: My go-to summer red—light to medium-bodied, smooth, and pretty. Pairs wonderfully with salmon, chicken marsala, and even dark chocolate.
- Malbec: Excellent with lamb, pork, or grilled meats with robust flavors.

- Chianti: A classic Italian red. Goes beautifully with tomato-based dishes, pizza, and charcuterie boards. Medium-bodied and dry.
- Sangria: Fruity, sweet, and refreshing—perfect for summer, brunch, or with tapas, blue cheeses, empanadas, and fish tacos.
- Rosé: I can't get enough. Wonderful with vegetables, seafood, salads, and creamy pasta dishes.
- Pinot Grigio: My favorite white—light, refreshing, and perfect chilled on a hot afternoon. Pairs well with fish, chicken, light pastas, and salads with goat cheese.

Quick Wine Tips

- A red blend is a simple, easy-drinking choice that goes well with gamey meats and beef.
- Chianti pairs with braised meats, rabbit, steak, and classic Italian cheeses.
- Cabernet Sauvignon is versatile for red meats and rich sauces.
- Pinot Noir is delicate enough for lighter dishes while still elegant.
- Sangria is a summer-friendly crowd-pleaser—fresh, fruity, and fun.
- Pinot Grigio is perfect for light, refreshing meals and alfresco dining.

Thank You!

To each and every one of you who has purchased this book, I pray this fills your heart and soul beyond measure. May it bring a smile to your face, may you find a meal you love, and may you share it with someone special. May it remind you of your own family memories. May you feel loved throughout the pages and be inspired to cook and create something amazing around your own table.

I surely couldn't leave out my sweet friend Rae Lesmeister—and of course her husband Tim, a man of many talents. Rae never let my dream die. If I put it aside when frustrated or overwhelmed, she was there to pull me out, to say, "You've got this." She inspired love, guided me, and did everything she could to see this book come to fruition—just as much as I did.

Oh, and always remember: use the fancy dishes, pour the good wine, don't be afraid to try something new, and make it your own. Take it up a notch. Never stop laughing, never stop loving.

Tina K ♡

About Tina K

I was born in East Islip, New York, and planted myself in sunny Florida in 1968. I've been soaking up all the sunshine and fun ever since. I'm married to my amazing husband, Drew, for 29 years (yes, he's survived me this long!) and I'm part of his chiropractic practice. I'm a proud mom to three incredible kids, a devoted dog mom, and—here's a fun tidbit—I used to be a Weeki Wachee mermaid. Yep, I performed as a real, live mermaid at Florida's world-famous attraction. Probably my favorite job ever. (Seriously, if you're in Florida, it's worth a visit just to say hi to the mermaids!)

I grew up in a big, loud, and loving Italian family. The chaos, the laughter, and the food-filled memories shaped me into the woman I am today, and I wouldn't trade it for the world. I have a ton of hobbies: swimming, paddleboarding, horseback riding, and creating beautiful spaces wherever I go (yes, even at the dinner table). My passions are simple but powerful: family, food, friends and sprinkling in a little of God's love into everything I do.

My goal in life? To bring joy, make a difference, brighten someone's day, and maybe turn a tough day into a little celebration. Life is too short not to eat, dance, laugh, and dream big.

So here's my advice: eat well, laugh often, dance like nobody's watching, and be the best you, every single day.

www.ingramcontent.com/pod-product-compliance
Ingram Content Group UK Ltd.
Pitfield, Milton Keynes, MK11 3LW, UK
UKRC032033290726
14090UKWH00007B/479